HAMMER AND PONDS

Relics of the Wealden Iron Industry

An introduction and guide

Helen Pearce

First published 2011
Revised 2012; reprinted 2015
Revised and reprinted 2018

Front cover: Fernhurst Furnace pond from the northern sluice
Back cover: Burton Forge Pond, near Petworth

Published by Pomegranate Press,
50 Bevernbridge Cottages, South Chailey, Lewes, Sussex BN8 4QB
pomegranatepress@aol.com
www.pomegranate-press.co.uk

ISBN: 978–1–907242–15–1

British Library Cataloguing-in-Publication Data.
A catalogue record for this book is available from the British Library

Printed and bound by 4 Edge Ltd, 7A Eldon Way, Hockley, Essex SS5 4AD

Dedicated to the memory of my mother,
Marlene Helen Patricia Pearce, 1938–1965

Oh, the hammer ponds of Sussex,
And the dewponds of the west,
Are part of Britain's heritage,
The part we love the best . . .

Acknowledgements

Many people and institutions helped with the research for this book. Above all I am indebted to the Wealden Iron Research Group, whose field walking and forays have yielded so much archaeological evidence of ironwork sites, as well as documentary research into their history and activities. WIRG's Jeremy Hodgkinson and the late Reg Houghton in particular deserve thanks for generously sharing specialist knowledge and making comments on the text. Any inaccuracies are mine, not theirs. Ron Martin of the Sussex Industrial Archaeology Society and Ted Henbery of Sussex Mills Group also kindly helped with information.

I am also very grateful to Robin and Carla Barnes of the Fernhurst Society for information regarding the furnace pond there, the late Roger Ray of Slaugham and his son Barry for details of Slaugham Furnace Pond and the chalybeate spring, James Masters for a guided tour and further details of Blackfold Furnace Pond, and those people who responded to my original queries on local internet newsgroups, such as Chris Shepheard of the Rural Life Centre, Tilford. For the diagram and other services I am indebted to Paperwork. I am very grateful to Louis Mackay for a swift execution of the map, and to Dave Revell for the original idea. Copyright has been sought assiduously: if an inadvertent breach has crept through I would be pleased to remedy this and provide acknowledgement in any future edition.

Local conservation groups and the Ramblers Association deserve praise for their admirable work in preserving and maintaining rights of way, footpaths and bridleways throughout the countryside, thus allowing easier access to such features.

Contents

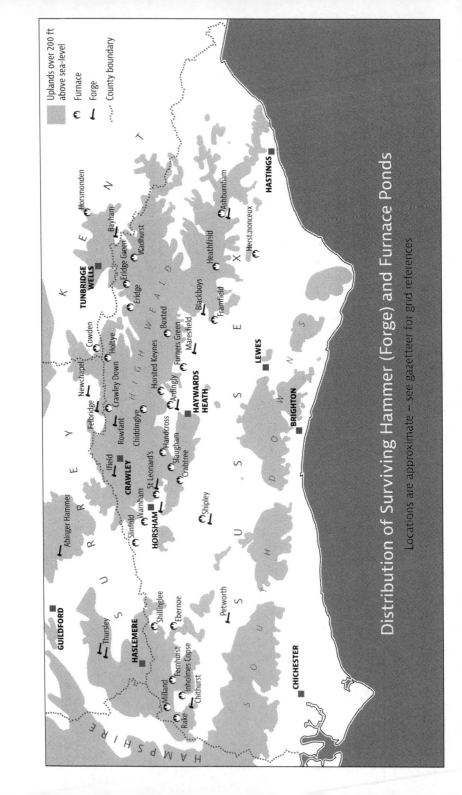

Distribution of Surviving Hammer (Forge) and Furnace Ponds

Locations are approximate – see gazetteer for grid references

Introduction

As a child I was intrigued by the term 'hammer lake' as my late Uncle Fred Howsego called Slaugham Pond in west Sussex: a frequent trip for a picnic or duck-feeding. A keen cyclist in his youth, he remembered several hammer lakes nearby. Years later, unable to recall the sites he mentioned, I investigated only to find innumerable references to hammer ponds and hammer woods all over the south-east. Most of the lakes are at least partially accessible, and blessed with an abundance of waterfowl and other wildlife, making for charming places to stop during a tour of the area. However, the historical origins of these waters were grimily practical rather than scenic or tranquil.

'Hammer' ponds are not natural lakes but dammed streams and rivers, crucial to the Tudor and Stuart iron industry based in the High Weald of Kent and Sussex, and adjacent parts of Surrey and Hampshire. The Weald was a major iron-producing region long before the Romans arrived, due to its abundant clay ironstone deposits. Smelting sites were determined by the quality of local ore, and the convenient location of other raw materials. These included naturally heat-resistant clay, later sandstone, to construct furnace hearths, and ample supplies of wood to make charcoal for fuel. Water was essential for cooling the iron and the High Weald enjoys many swift streams in deep, densely wooded valleys, known locally as 'ghylls', which eventually played a pivotal role. From the end of the fifteenth century new developments in the smelting industry ensured some ghylls were impounded and the heads of water that built up drove 'iron mill' waterwheels. These powered huge furnace bellows and forge hammers to pound the new pig iron into refined bars.

Occasionally references to these ponds or the iron industry appear in popular literature, such as the Sussex novels of Sheila Kaye-Smith and Barbara Willard, W. Victor Cook's *Forges in the Forest*, Conan Doyle's *Adventure of Black Peter*, and of course Kipling's *Puck of Pook's Hill*, set near Burwash. Of the handful of Victorian novels based around ironworks families, the most famous is probably George E. Sargent's *Hurlock Chase*, which includes fairly accurate accounts of furnace operation by an author who claimed to have known some elderly local iron-masters in his youth. A more unusual tribute to the industry is the rare 'Sussex Forge' variety of apple that once flourished in West Sussex, allegedly named after the old hammer forges around the East Grinstead area. Hammer ponds occasionally feature on old scenic postcards of the Weald yet with little clue as to their past function.

This guide draws on two major historical and topographical sources, namely E. Straker's *Wealden Iron* (1931) and H. Cleere and D. Crossley's *The Iron Industry of the Weald* [C&C] (1995). C&C includes gazetteers of all known bloomeries and later furnaces and forges, gathered from the continuing investigations of the Wealden Iron Research Group [WIRG]. The annual WIRG Bulletin provides recent reports and their online iron site database is updated constantly (see **Industrial History Societies** below).

Wealden Iron – A Brief History

Early iron smelting

The Weald's iron deposits lie relatively close to the ground surface, and so were easily extracted by open cast mining. Most extraction and smelting took place in the High Weald, an area stretching roughly east of Horsham across to south of Tunbridge Wells, and down to Hastings. High yields were obtained within this geological triangle: beneath the Wadhurst Clay in the Hastings Beds, and in parts of the Weald Clay and Tunbridge Wells Sand. The great forests of Worth, St Leonard's and Ashdown had early been important smelting districts, systematically managed by multi-stemmed coppicing to conserve timber for charcoal production.

The earliest, rudimentary, form of iron smelting is known as the 'direct' or bloomery process. A small conical furnace, located close to an iron ore source, was built of clay, in which iron ore was smelted with burning charcoal. The temperature was boosted by draughts from leather bellows, pumped by hand or foot, through pipes into the furnace base. Charcoal not only generates a higher and more consistent temperature than wood, but also produces carbon monoxide during combustion, further assisting the chemical reduction of ore particles. As gases escaped through an outlet in the clay roof, and waste material ran down and away, the molten iron was reduced to a malleable lump at the base of the bloomery.

This iron lump, or 'bloom', contained a high degree of cinder, so had to be purified or 'reduced' further by hammering into a solid bar, weighing between ten and twenty pounds, or forged immediately into tools or weapons. The bloomery was a relatively wasteful method as discarded cinders contained much residual iron oxide. It is these accumulations, and other debris in the ground, that aid the detection of early smelting areas. Bloomeries were usually sited near streams whose high banks exposed geological seams, allowing the easy identification of adequate iron ore, and therefore the best prospecting sites. Streams provided water to cool the iron and forge tools, but water power wasn't used for any part of this extremely laborious and thirsty process.

Water Power and Blast Furnaces

Methods changed little until the twelfth century. Continental bloomeries then increased production dramatically by harnessing power from rapid streams to turn waterwheels, along similar lines to grain and other mills. Cams on a central wheelshaft lifted open bigger bellows, which then fell via a counterweight. This mechanism was obviously far more powerful than pumping by hand, and the stronger draughts piped or 'blasted' into the furnace allowed a much bigger bloomery to work for longer periods. Yet little information survives about the Wealden iron industry during the medieval period, apart from its trade in blooms for smiths, nails, hinges, wheel-strakes, miscellaneous materials for royal and church buildings, and weaponry. Given the relative paucity of documentary and field evidence it remains unclear where early water-powered bloomery forges were situated (Chingley, and Roughy near Horsham, are possibilities) or whether they produced pig or bar iron.

Meanwhile on the Continent, bigger, permanent 'blast' furnaces were developed, typically square stone towers, approximately seven metres square and six metres high, their shafts lined with brick or fire-resistant clay. Furnace hearths were also constructed of sandstone, to withstand intense heat without cracking, or attracting a thick layer of waste iron. Such accretions could solidify and block the furnace. A short shaft of about two feet wide combined the functions of fuel inlet and chimney where vapours could escape. Banks or bridges were built up the side of the furnace for access ramps to feed or charge this shaft with ore and charcoal. Limestone was added as a flux, which aided ore reduction and the removal of impurities from the finished product. Clustered around the furnace stack were roofed 'lean-to' structures housing the bellows apparatus, the tapping outlet and casting pits. Cranes were erected next to the

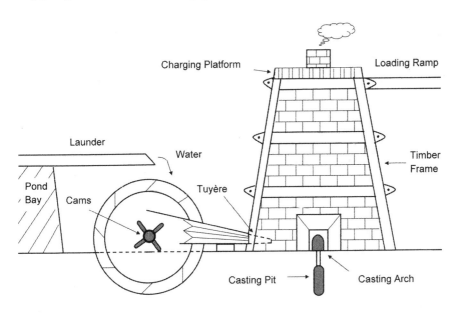

Simplified diagram of a blast furnace (not to scale). Waterwheel and tailrace are to the rear of stack. Roofs to casting and bellows sheds have been omitted.

gun-casting pits, and both furnaces and forges required numerous other sheds to store fuel, tools, and shelter workers.

Once alight, the new improved furnace stayed 'in blast' for a much longer period of time than the old bloomeries. A new hearth had to be built for every smelting 'campaign', which could last several months (C&C, 1995: 221). Any sudden stoppage would choke the furnace with partially smelted ore and solidified cast iron, causing irreversible damage (Herbert, 1985: 31). Higher temperatures consistently maintained in blast furnaces liquefied the iron to the extent that it could be tapped straight into sand

Model of hammer and helve plus the original hammer head from Etchingham Forge, Anne of Cleves House Museum (by kind permission of the Sussex Archaeological Society).

furrows to form long 'sow' bars (which could weigh up to half a ton) branching into smaller 'pigs', or poured into moulds for other items. Mass production was now possible, as output reached industrial quantities: to up to a ton of molten iron per day, with far less iron lost in waste slag.

Pig iron was brittle due to the high carbon content absorbed from the charcoal. Remelting and hammering at a finery forge was required to convert it into highly durable wrought iron. Larger forges were now built with waterwheels both to power bellows for the hearths, yielding even higher temperatures, and to drive mechanical hammers that pounded iron into short bars or anconies. The hammer's cast-iron head was set upon a wooden beam, or 'helve'. Again, the wheelshaft lifted the helve via cams to drop the hammer on the anvil continually, up to 60 blows per minute, far faster than manual hammering. Anconies were forged further in chafery hearths where they were re-heated, hammered and trimmed into malleable bars for smiths. This three-stage conversion or 'indirect' process, pioneered in the Low Countries, was known as the Walloon system. Conversion forges dramatically increased production. They were sited at some distance from the furnace, but usually along the same stream.

The High Weald's natural advantages made it the ideal location to experiment with the new methods. The first British blast furnace was built around 1490 at Queenstock in the Buxted area, but little documentary evidence about this enterprise has survived. By 1496 Henry VII sought state of the art weapons for his impending campaign against Scotland. He invited French ironworkers from the Pays de Bray in Normandy, an area of iron-smelting expertise, to cast here using the Walloon system. Bray lies within what was geologically speaking 'Wealden'

France before the formation of the Channel. Many skilled immigrants arrived from this region over the next fifty years or more, and much of the original French terminology endured, eg 'chafery', and 'tuyere' (ie the clay pipes for the bellows). This pioneer work was arguably the first British industrial revolution, starting nearly seventy years before the birth of the Midlands blast furnace industry.

Other furnaces were soon set up near Buxted and the Ashdown Forest area, such as Newbridge and at Hartfield. Newbridge's initial products included pig iron, shot, and cast-iron gun carriages (C&C, 95: 113) but the increased output enabled relatively easy development and manufacture of large guns. As part of the military impetus, the first Wealden cannon were soon cast, in two parts. While cheaper than bronze cannon these were less reliable due to a relatively poor seal. The existing wrought-iron cannon design, consisting of iron staves bonded with hoops, continued in use for some decades. Incidentally, it was these older style guns, not Wealden cannon, which were found on Henry VIII's ill-fated Mary Rose.

Sussex gun founding was revitalized fifty years later when Parson William Levett, gunstone maker to the Crown, inherited his brother's furnaces around Buxted, including Queenstock. There, in 1543, he employed Frenchman Peter Baude from the Houndsditch foundry in London. Bronze guns were cast in one piece at Houndsditch and Baude now cast Sussex iron in vertical gun pit moulds, muzzle uppermost. This prevented air or slag pockets and so increased structural strength and reliability (Herbert, 1985: 58). The iron was poured around a model of the cannon bore and the aperture was later smoothed out or 'reamed' precisely at a boring-mill by a revolving cutting bar. The bar was also driven by a waterwheel, usually near the furnace, sometimes on a tributary stream. Reliable, durable Sussex guns were now available. Not all furnaces were able to produce guns, nevertheless within a century of Queenstock's innovations over a hundred blast furnaces and associated fineries were operating in the Weald. From the late sixteenth century other parts of Britain near suitable ore deposits started building similar ironworks.

There are a few sketchy contemporary pictures of these ironworks. We can get a better idea of the external appearance and mechanics of the furnace from the (half scale) replica recently built at the Rural Life Centre, Tilford (see Museums) and even the Lenard fireback (below). Further clues can be obtained from photographs of preserved later furnace buildings elsewhere in Riden's (1993) gazetteer of blast furnaces throughout Britain (see References).

Half-size replica furnace stack (by kind permission of the Rural Life Centre, Tilford).

On the technical side, Swedish theologist and scientist Emanuel Swedenborg published a diagrammatic cross-section of the internal 'inverted bottle' structure of Lamberhurst's Gloucester Furnace stack in 1734.

Anne of Cleves House Museum in Lewes, East Sussex, has an extensive exhibition of the entire iron-making process, including estimates of the raw materials required. Eight wagonloads of wood produced 2.5 loads of charcoal, which could smelt 2.5 tons of iron ore. Most blast furnaces could produce over 200 tons of iron per year, either in the form of pig iron or various products including ordnance.

Wealden cannon were inspected for quality and tested or 'proved', to reject any with potentially lethal manufacturing faults. Some test firing took place locally, and iron cannon balls continue to be uncovered occasionally in grassy banks near old furnace sites. Guns for government ordnance or sale to foreign governments

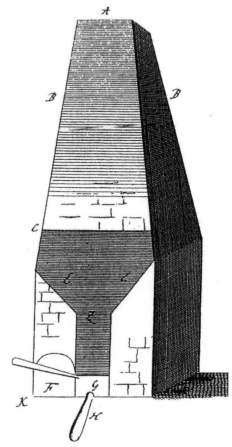

Emanuel Swedenborg's 1734 cross-section of Gloucester Furnace, Lamberhurst: G represents the hearth, H the orifice for tapping iron. The tuyere pipe for the bellows is just above F.

were sent to Woolwich Arsenal to be proved by Crown inspectors. Sussex guns were renowned for their reliability unlike some foreign cannon which occasionally exploded when fired. Cheaper and lighter than bronze cannon, their weight still caused some problems on ships but not in static positions at the proliferating southern coastal forts and defences. Illicit exports by cannon dealers to foreign powers occasionally resulted in their use by the enemy, despite legislation prohibiting such sales. Britain's increasing overseas trade, colonial endeavours and other skirmishes further sustained this market.

Rapid fortunes could be made from iron founding. Rich landowners and farmers soon established ironworks on their own land or elsewhere as appropriate, hiring skilled ironworkers. Major iron families included famous Wealden names such as the Challoners, Bowyers, Carylls, the Streatfeildes of Chiddingstone, the Fullers of Brightling and the Barhams of Wadhurst. Many expanded and built more than one furnace or forge, accumulating

The Mayfield Gun, High Street, Mayfield.

17

considerable wealth, which funded opulent estates such as the Infields' Gravetye Manor. Innumerable more modest but nevertheless luxurious homes, like the Bakers' timber-framed Middle House in Mayfield, sprang up around the iron estates and villages. Many skilled ironworkers prospered, and in turn invested in the industry themselves, renting land and waters, and subsequently enjoyed considerable social mobility. The title of 'ironmaster' is consequently ambiguous, as it might refer to the financier, the landowner, or the site's clerk of works. An increased need for allied trades such as carters, hauliers and shippers also boosted the local economy.

Cinder waste had long been recycled to surface the frequently waterlogged clay roads, but now these Wealden highways were increasingly busy. New tracks had to be built down to relatively remote ironworks, sometimes over surviving portions of old Roman roads, and it was important they could support heavy loads of fuel and iron drawn by oxen. The new smelting system required far greater supplies of charcoal from surrounding woodland, as much as 5000 tons in a year. The iron industry, among others, was often blamed for the deforestation of the Weald – which remains one of the most densely wooded areas in Britain – but with few exceptions, ironmasters were conscientious about coppicing and replanting woodlands to replenish supplies.

Hammer and Furnace Ponds

Although old ironworks lakes are often referred to as hammer ponds, by now it should be obvious that a hammer pond served a forge, not a furnace. Confusion is perhaps inevitable given that the two enterprises were often connected by owner and location.

Moreover, the design for forge or furnace water supplies was virtually identical. A large dam was built across a valley to impound an existing stream. While this usually consisted mainly of sandy soil and clay, a fixed core of timber piles or even sandstone blocks has been discovered in a few excavations. The bank was then reinforced with furnace slag underneath a waterproof clay top layer, and finally covered with topsoil and turf. A mixture of slag and topsoil was also used to raise the level of the embankment later, if necessary. The term 'bay' for dams derived from early building measurements used by carpenters, who were also the original specialists in dam-construction for mills (Binnie, 1987: 13).

Furnace or forge buildings were sited below the bay, which raised the water level by ten or fifteen feet to build up water pressure. This was released through a sluice to an overshot waterwheel driven by the weight of water falling into the buckets. At around fifteen inches wide this was narrower than a corn mill wheel, yet its economical use of water could drive two pairs of bellows at a furnace. A tailrace carried the used water away from the wheel and back to the stream but was usually culverted and always positioned well away from the casting pits. Any water seeping underneath a furnace would have turned to steam and caused a lethal explosion.

Spillways, or overflows, were built some distance away and usually at that end of the bay nearest the original stream bed. These served to prevent inundations when pond levels ran high. Reliable water management systems were essential, yet as silt built up both flow and storage capacity gradually diminished, so 'pen' or feeder ponds were often constructed upstream to provide emergency supplies to top up the main pond. Many pen ponds survive where the main ponds have not.

An alternative reservoir method at some sites used a long channel from a stream tributary to supplement the main water source. Iridge Furnace at Hurst Green, Sussex, had a complex arrangement of thirty relatively small ponds, linked by sluices. Without these, sited in an exceptionally narrow valley, the furnace would have required unfeasibly high bays to hoard enough water (Hodgkinson & Houghton, 2000: 34). Water shortages threatened not only continuity of production but also the furnace structure: if the temperature got too low the iron solidified inside the stack and the whole furnace might have to be rebuilt. This risk ensured treading the wheel was an arduous and expensive necessity during periods of low rainfall or drought when completion of ordnance or other orders could not be delayed. Blasting campaigns therefore took place in the winter months when water should be plentiful, ensuring a constant powerful flow. Forges also needed large quantities of water as they could use up to four waterwheels on two or more tailraces to operate perhaps two hammers and finery and chafery hearths (Hodgkinson, 2008: 59), but their ponds usually had time to refill overnight.

The legal right to impound streams was obviously crucial for any ironworks, yet suitable land and furnace or forge buildings were often leased from landowners by tenant ironmasters. Conflict occasionally erupted, usually fuelled by tenancy disputes. Denise Bowyer, lessee of the important Parrock Forge near Hartfield in the early sixteenth century, suffered extensive damage to her business when her new landlord William Saunders claimed possession. His men broke up her ponds and assaulted her workers, cutting off one man's finger. Rallying forces armed with staves, bills and bows and arrows, she made a violent counter attack, but the outcome is not recorded (Straker, 1931: 243).

Given the obvious difficulties in transporting and keeping sea fish many large estates built fishponds stocked with fresh-water fish. These valuable supplies became a profitable sideline for ironworks ponds, but could also cause discord. Nicholas Fowle of Riverhall Furnace was enjoined to provide his landlord, the rector of Rotherfield, with fifty per cent of his annual catch as part payment for having constructed a pond on church land (Wright, 1982: 53). In 1587 at Gosden Furnace, St Leonard's Forest, landlord Edward Caryll and lessee Roger Gratwick argued over fishing rights, escalating an existing row about the tenancy into another violent clash. About twenty of Caryll's servants fought and wounded Gratwick's workforce before stealing quantities of iron ore for Caryll's own furnace at Shipley (Straker, 1931: 438). Other attacks took place before Gratwick finally lost the lease to this furnace.

Conflict also arose when ironworks fouled the water or interrupted supply to other iron or grain mills downstream. Local flooding could occur when ponds overflowed or severe storms breached bays or burst spillways, thereby damaging fields and roads, and fines were imposed.

Furnaces and water-powered forges were potentially hazardous places and injuries were not uncommon, yet there were surprisingly few recorded deaths within the workplaces themselves. Ponds, as with other industrial and agricultural water supplies, posed a regular threat and not just to workers. In 1629 unfortunate traveller Richard Heather drowned when his horse leapt into the pond having been startled by the noise of a furnace near Iping. The coroner noted "the closeness of the furnace to the road and the depth of the water in the pond" (Hunnisett, 1998: 76). Iron founder Nicholas Jerrat's three-year-old son accidentally fell into Horsmonden/Brenchley Furnace pond in 1592 (Zell, 1994: 131), and later in 1683 another "wayfarer", Edward Kendall, also drowned there (Edwards, 1996: 162).

Wealden Products

Blast furnaces now obviously focused on producing larger iron products, ie pig and bar iron for sale to local smiths and London ironmongers, until cannon dominated production. The weight of such items and the fragile road conditions usually necessitated shipping them to London via the nearest navigable rivers such as the Medway, or down the Rother and Brede to the sea ports of Rye, Hastings and Newhaven, or the iron warehouses at Pevensey sluice. Cargoes leaving Channel seaports were always vulnerable to the possibility of marauding foreign ships.

Other, smaller, output continued to include builders' sundries, nails, wheel-rims, ploughshares and other agricultural tools, and domestic items for open hearths. Perhaps most famous are the cast-iron Wealden firebacks and 'grave slabs', a lucrative sideline. Iron memorial slabs, produced mainly to commemorate ironmasters' family members rather than the nobility, can be found within many local 'iron village' churches eg at Chiddingstone, Cowden, Horsmonden, Mayfield, Salehurst, Sedlescombe, and West Hoathly. These were usually set into the floors, not necessarily over a grave as such, but unfortunately carpet or pews now cover some. The church of St Peter and St Paul in Wadhurst has the most extensive and remarkable collection of over thirty grave slabs on view, many embossed with the family coat of arms, including those of the Barhams, and there are two iron tombstones in the churchyard. The largest iron grave slab lies far from the Weald in Streat

22

Church near Ditchling, commemorating Martha and Elizabeth Gott, wife and daughter respectively of Peter Gott, owner of Gloucester furnace at Lamberhurst where the slab was cast.

Grave slabs and firebacks were made by tapping molten iron into sand moulds, previously impressed with a design from carved wooden boards, known as stamps. Firebacks protected the rear brick wall in fireplaces from heat, and their design changed to a narrower but taller shape after coal became a popular fuel during the eighteenth century. Decorative edges were sometimes added to firebacks by pressing a piece of twisted rope around the mould. Most slabs and firebacks boasted initials, heraldic symbols or classical scenes, while

Iron memorial to John Bottinge of Bower Forge, St Mary Magdalene Church, Cowden (by kind permission of the Diocese of Chichester).

Iron Graveslab, St Peter & St Paul Church, Wadhurst
(by kind permission of the church)

24

periodic fashions included biblical stories and political themes (Hodgkinson, 2010). Many can be seen in old houses open to the public, such as Bateman's and Michelham Priory, East Sussex and Lullingstone Castle, Kent, or even the occasional hotel or pub fireplace. Some are reproductions, cast in moulds from the originals, which can nevertheless be very old. There is an impressive display of original firebacks at Anne of Cleves House Museum in Lewes, among them the famous Lenard fireback of 1636, which depicts ironmaster Richard Lenard of Brede, his furnace stack, various ironworkers' tools, and his dog.

Another (*overleaf*) commemorates the Sussex Protestant martyrs, shown bound together at the stake, and there is a fireback celebrating the accession of James I. A later popular pattern was the 'Royal Oak' in which Charles II hid during his flight after the battle of Worcester in 1651.

The Lenard fireback (by kind permission of the Sussex Archaeological Society)

The Lewes Martyrs fireback (by kind permission of the Sussex Archaeological Society)

For those interested in the many fireback designs, Hodgkinson's *British Cast-Iron Firebacks* (2010) catalogues these and charts their history. More Wealden iron articles can also be viewed at the Priest House in West Sussex, and various local museums (see Museums below). Relatively small local iron products produced later than the early 1800s are often erroneously described as Wealden iron. However to the extent that scrap iron was recycled and continuously remelted at forges and foundries, it is likely that many such items contain small quantities of genuine Wealden iron.

Wrought-iron balustrades and screens were manufactured for wealthier houses and churches, some of which are still *in situ*, such as the attractive iron screens across the chancel at Ashburnham church (TQ 695164). Gloucester Furnace at Lamberhurst in Kent cast the old gates and railings for St Paul's Cathedral around 1710: this required 200 tons of iron and cost more than £11,000. Some are still in place at the cathedral but most were removed: there are sections in the gun garden at

Lewes Castle, and on the pavement near the car park in Lamberhurst village. The gates of Reigate Priory in Surrey (TQ 254498) were also forged from Sussex iron. More unusually, the stocks and whipping post by Ninfield Green in East Sussex (TQ 707124) were cast locally in the seventeenth century, probably at Ashburnham.

During the English Civil War most ironworks supplied wholesale ironmongers with bar iron and thereby distanced themselves somewhat from the consequences, but a few owners armed either side and became involved in the conflict. Royalist ironworks in St Leonard's Forest were destroyed by Colonel Sir William Waller's Parliamentarian forces in the 1640s (C&C, 1995: 183).

Furnaces were easily restored as long as the ponds were in good condition, but fluctuating ordnance demands ensured that iron fortunes ebbed or flowed with peace or war. During the former the industry was sustained by gun founding for the merchant trade such as the East India Company, and export, as well as producing smaller items.

St Paul's Railings, Lewes Castle Gun Garden (by permission of the Sussex Archaeological Society)

Daniel Defoe described the ironworks he encountered when passing through the Weald in 1722:

'... at which they cast great quantities of iron cauldrons, chimney-backs, furnaces, retorts, boiling pots, and all such necessary things of iron; besides iron cannon, bomb-shells, stink-pots, hand grenadoes, and cannon ball, &c. in an infinite quantity . . .' (Defoe, 1986: 165).

Over 14,000 Wealden guns were cast overall. Many survive at various locations, including artillery museums at Leeds, Woolwich, and Fort Nelson in Portsmouth, and other forts and

The Pevensey Gun, (by kind permission of English Heritage)

Ninfield stocks

castles including Tilbury, Portland Castle, and the Tower of London. There is a sixteenth century demi-culverin cannon, with Elizabeth I's cypher on the barrel, within the grounds of Pevensey Castle. The Mayfield Cannon, on display in Mayfield High Street, was cast locally by Sir Thomas Gresham circa 1567–79. Wealden cannon can also found at garrisons in former colonies, such as St. Lucia, Barbados, and Antigua. The identification of early Wealden guns is not easy, involving such variables as length, royal cyphers, the shape of the cascabels, and the manufacturer's mark. Such a 'trade' mark usually consists of initials, such as IF or JF for John Fuller, A for Ashburnham or G for Gloucester (Lamberhurst), cast in relief on the trunnions. However this device was not widely used in Britain before the early eighteenth century (Brown, 1989: 321). A rare example of a gun with the Commonwealth cypher can be seen at Fort Nelson.

The End of Wealden Iron

After 1650 cheap Swedish bar iron imports seriously undercut Wealden iron prices. Local furnaces focused even more on lucrative gunfounding, while the surviving forges mainly worked up surplus or scrap iron from furnace castings. Despite the preservation of timber supplies, additional demand for fuel from the clothmaking, glass, brick, and hop industries made charcoal increasingly expensive. The search for a cheaper yet reliable alternative began. Coal is not suitable for iron smelting as the high sulphur content renders the iron too brittle, but Abraham Darby of Shropshire finally succeeded in converting coal into far less sulphurous coke by 1709. This comparatively inexpensive fuel increased the volume of iron production, especially after the perfection of an atmospheric steam engine, which eradicated the old problem of sustaining water supplies during dry seasons (Straker, 1931: 65).

Remote from coal sources, competing with cheaper pig and bar iron at home and imports from abroad, Wealden furnaces declined irretrievably over the eighteenth century, despite a boost during the Seven Years' War of 1756-63, and before the Napoleonic Wars were anticipated. In 1764 the Weald lost naval contracts to the Carron Ironworks in Scotland, blessed with a nearby coalmine and therefore cheap coke, and improved gun designs soon rendered Wealden gunfounding methods obsolete. Most Wealden ironworks had closed by the end of the eighteenth century, resulting in considerable unemployment. Ashburnham Furnace in East Sussex was the last to cease production in 1813, bringing over three hundred years of the blast furnace industry to a close.

Disappointingly for many industrial archaeologists, only the old bays and some of the 'hammer lakes', both easily mistaken for natural phenomena, provide obvious visual clues to former ironworks. No Wealden furnace structures survived because components such as bricks and cast-iron scraps were reclaimed and reused for other building projects. Outbuildings around the stack varied in size and height. Forges had fewer, smaller structures than furnaces, making these sites even more difficult to identify in fieldwork.

Some of the original masonry around spillways remains on a few bays, although much was replaced in subsequent centuries. Dry hollows and ditches on embankments are often a clue to former wheelpits and sluices but these can be difficult to spot among the undergrowth. Residual mounds of furnace slag spoil are long covered by turf, but pieces of black glassy slag can often be found embedded in the paths nearby. Portable objects found at the sites have long been removed to museums, but for those wishing to see any structural foundations and features that remain *in situ* the best sites to visit are Fernhurst Furnace and Ashburnham. The latter's main ponds are dry, but enough relevant clues survive in the valley there to make for an interesting walk.

Surviving Ponds

Over 180 furnaces and associated forges operated within the Weald between the fifteenth and nineteenth century, each with its own pond, and usually a few pen ponds. Most of these are

The spillway at Ashburnham Furnace bay with some original masonry.

now dry. Some were drained and the land reclaimed for agricultural use. Crops such as hops particularly enjoyed the rich silty soil of these fields. A few ponds were swallowed up by reservoirs such as Ardingly, Darwell and Bewl, or covered by industrial or housing estates. Tilgate Furnace Pond now lies beneath the suburb of Furnace Green, south of Crawley. Tilgate Lake nearby (TQ 279345) is the largest of a few possible pen ponds that served the furnace, now within Tilgate Forest Park. Many ponds were converted to serve grain mills, others reclaimed as ornamental lakes in private grounds with the original bays considerably altered or destroyed.

Dozens of hammer and furnace ponds remain however in the High Weald between the North and South Downs, especially in mid Sussex. Usually hidden within wooded valleys, most are well worth visiting. They attract and support a variety of waterfowl, dragonflies and amphibians amongst the rushes and water lilies and several lie within designated nature reserves. Some are now private fishing lakes.

Local place names, such as Hammer Stream, Cinder Plat or Mine Pits Field are obvious clues to previous iron-workings in an area. However cinder can also refer to bloomery sites. Given the earlier proliferation of bloomeries over the Weald it is said that few Sussex fields don't contain any cinder. After ore extraction was exhausted mine pits were filled in, but as these settled craters often formed, filling with water. These should not be confused with furnace or hammer ponds, nor should marlpits. Marling was an old agricultural practice where clay was used as an alkaline top-dressing to improve the acidic local soil. Digging for marl could expose iron ore and vice versa, so excavations were often combined.

A few furnace or forge water features survive in part only and so are not included in the main gazetteer. Unusually, Gloucester Furnace near Lamberhurst (TQ 662360) was not powered by a pond, but by a particularly deep section of the River Teise redirected into a specially constructed 800-yard leat to the furnace. This (now dry) channel, known as the Hoathly Ditch, is on private land, but visible from a footpath from the B2169 west of Lamberhurst. At Ashurst in Kent there is an interesting series of ponds and channels along the west bank of what was once Ashurst Forge (TQ 507391) but it remains unclear whether these were related to the forge. Recently a fragment of Etchingham Forge Pond, believed destroyed when the railway was built across its bed, was found along with evidence of previous leats near the river Rother (TQ 701266) (Herbert & Cornish, 2012: 28).

'Pond Bays' of defunct ironworks are often clearly marked as antiquities on Ordnance Survey maps of the Weald, like those on streams around Brightling and Dallington in East Sussex and Mayfield in Kent. Relatively few still hold water as ponds. Don't be misled: the broken bay for Beech Furnace is marked and lies on Wadhurst Lane, near Battle (TQ 728167) but a pond close by is not that of the old ironworks. Extensive details of all known iron-working sites and their relics, such as mills, wheelpits, broken bays, spillways, weirs, and leats can be found in Cleere and Crossley and on WIRG's online database.

The remaining ponds cannot hint at the widespread heavy industry and associated relative population density that dominated the scene centuries ago. Mine pits scarred much of the landscape. Blast furnaces and hammer forges required large quantities of ore, timber, charcoal, pig iron and other weighty products to be hauled over long distances, rutting and churning the muddy rural roads, which often became impassable at least during winter. Ironmasters were occasionally fined for this, and they were legally enjoined to spread slag and cinder over highways in return for transporting heavy freight. They often bequeathed money for the continuing repair of roads (Straker, 1931: 184) as well as philanthropic – and grandiloquent – gestures. The varied interests, escapades and intermarriages of the great iron families, owners and lessees, are interesting in themselves and would fill another book. Some of their biographies are included in Teesdale's (1991) work on the economics of sixteenth century gun founding and Hodgkinson's (2008) history of the Wealden iron industry.

The clamour of the hammers, the acrid smoke from the furnaces, the countless miners, fillers, finers, hammermen and

The grass meadow bed of the former Ashburnham Furnace Pond.

carters, the roads blocked by oxen hauling iron and fuel, and riverboats laden with bar iron would have presented a far busier and noisier landscape than today's peaceful waters. Weed and silt have reduced some ponds in size while others have been altered and even enlarged for ornamental purposes. All have been reclaimed by flora and fauna, and many are now within or adjacent to sites of special scientific interest (SSSIs).

Often assumed to be natural beauty spots in the High Weald (now an Area of Outstanding Natural Beauty) these delightful artificial lakes are useful reminders of the largely concealed *post-industrial* nature of so much of our countryside.

Blast furnace slag (here from the Sow Track at Ashburnham) is often found on paths around furnace sites.

Gazetteer of Surviving Ponds

This gazetteer lists surviving furnace or forge ponds, including reclaimed ornamental sites, plus a few large pen ponds. For brevity's sake it includes the approximate term of a site's working life, where known, rather than the various stoppages and changes of ownership. Most work areas have been destroyed or covered by earth and vegetation, and some bays have been rebuilt, even slightly repositioned, over the years and so are not original. Grid references below therefore provide the main access to the ponds, which is not necessarily the exact site of former furnace or forge working areas. The origins of some sites' names are now obscure. To ease location, ponds are listed according to the nearest village or town rather than administrative boundary, and the relevant Ordnance Survey Explorer map number is provided. Thanks to the internet, the most isolated locations can now be viewed online using satellite images (although the ponds themselves are sometimes obscured by trees).

Few ponds are signposted, but most are at least partially accessible from a footpath. These are often near long distance paths, such as the Sussex Border Path or the High Weald Landscape Trail. Robust walkers can therefore enjoy the ponds as part of longer walks. Such routes can occasionally be found in the leisure sections of local newspapers and websites. Railway stations are mentioned where there is one within a couple of miles. A few bus routes pass nearby, but a walk is still usually necessary along minor roads and footpaths. I strongly recommend walkers obtain a local bus map, and check current routes and times before setting out.

People with restricted mobility will be disappointed to learn that there are rarely suitable or convenient places to park nearby: exceptions are noted. Many ponds lurk down muddy rugged footpaths, sometimes far from the road. A few sites are wheelchair accessible (allegedly: some struck me as rather rough terrain) and only for a short distance around the site. Again, these are mentioned below. It might be said that all lakes look the same, but each has its own special characteristics in a specific setting. I hope it is clear which ponds are impressive enough to travel some distance to enjoy, and those, eg the partially visible Hamsell and Riverhall, which merit a visit only if you are already in the vicinity.

Please note: most ponds are on or near private property but at least accessible to view from a footpath. I've indicated where ponds can be seen from public rights of way. Some cannot. Please do not trespass.

Readers may be surprised and even disappointed by the omission of some well known 'hammer ponds'. The ponds near Pophole Forge in Surrey, by the county border at Hammer Vale, are modern fishing lakes. The forge pond is long gone although the dressed stone spillway remains on the stream at SU 874326. Shottermill Ponds, near Haslemere, are often described as old pen ponds for Pophole. There is no evidence to support this, or that Oliver's corn mill on 'Three Counties Bridge' was an iron mill site.

Imbhams Furnace Pond, just west of Haslemere at SU 932329 is dry: one might easily confuse this with the large pond at nearby Imbhams Farm, which has no connections with the old ironworks. However, part of Imbhams Furnace's boring-mill pond survives about a mile north of Furnace Place at 929355. Vachery Forge and Furnace sites are dry, close to but not beneath the great Vachery Lake constructed in 1814 to feed the Wey and Arun canal. The eroded Vachery Forge pond bay can be seen along part of the public footpath at Hammer Farm (TQ 062370).

Excavations have also revealed that beautiful Lurgashall Mill Pond did not power Lurgashall Furnace: the original bay is at Old Mill Farm (SU 942261), now dry and marked as an antiquity on the OS map. Horam Manor Farm, south of Heathfield, has several ponds on different levels. These are not proven to be hammer or furnace ponds but former mine pits, originally dug for Waldron Furnace to the northeast, and also for marl. They were later enlarged and converted into fishponds. Hollywater Pond in east Hampshire, Friday Street Mill in Surrey, and the Longford Stream near Chailey in East Sussex have all been described as hammer ponds. There is no documentary or field evidence of a hammer forge at these sites.

Although the Wealden clay extends slightly into east Hampshire, there is no definite record of furnaces operating that far over in the northwest Weald. Local water-powered forges imported pig iron from Sussex. Bramshott Hammer Forge near Liphook, established in 1590, was converted to a paper mill around 1690, known as Passfield. The site (SU 819344) is now covered by industrial development and the surviving water channels were created for the paper mill. Waggoner's Wells ponds near Grayshott, built by Henry Hooke, tenant of Bramshott Forge, are often described as hammer or pen ponds but are downstream of Bramshott Hammer and never served a forge. Hampshire followed the Weald's example and developed several ironworks in the southwest of the county, using non-Wealden sources of ore such as Hengistbury Head, or scrap, but their history is beyond this scope of this book.

Physical identification of former hammer or furnace ponds

can be difficult, particularly when the buildings and waters were reused for other mills such as gunpowder, grain or paper, after iron production ceased. Iron mills' bay construction methods were reliable and imitated when building ornamental ponds in private parks. Occasionally smaller ponds are rumoured to have dried up or mysteriously reappear. Recent changes or discoveries may not be covered in this guide. WIRG's on-going fieldwork may yet identify more ponds, or disqualify some. They are always pleased to welcome new members to their forays.

Safety note: All paths are muddier, and a few impassable, after rain, rendering some sites hazardous. Please take care, especially with children, as few accessible ponds are fenced. Photography is difficult where trees and brushwood obstruct the view but always watch your step.

Finally, respect the local wildlife and remember the Country Code.

Gazetteer symbols:

Ex   Ordnance Survey Explorer map
ACC   Sites open to the public
PV   Private sites viewable from a public road or path
P   Private property – no access
NT   National Trust site
SSSI   Site of Special Scientific Interest
    Wheelchair access

West Sussex

Ardingly

TQ 337287

Ex 135

SSSI

ACC

Station: Balcombe

The earliest reference to Ardingly Forge is 1559. Owned by Francis Challoner, it operated until around 1696. The site was soon reused as a fulling mill, but this area now lies beneath the reservoir here. A much reduced Ardingly Furnace Pond, however, also established by Challoner circa 1592, survives at Great Saucelands. This can be reached by a footpath east of the reservoir's own bay, by the main car park. The reservoir is down a track from College Road, a minor road off the B2028 south of Crawley to Ardingly. There is an activity centre for water sports, car park and disabled car park nearer the water. Light refreshments. Tel: 01444 892549

Chiddinglye Woods, West Hoathly

TQ 346318

Ex 135

SSSI

PV

Established by Thomas Mitchell circa 1546, Chittingly Manor Furnace Pond lies within Chiddinglye Woods on private land.

However, one of its pen ponds is accessible and another visible from a slippery path and bridleway, which runs east from the Ardingly/Turners Hill road (B2028) near Wakehurst Place. The paths follow a bridge over the stream which broadens into a chain of pen ponds still on private land but just visible from the eastward path when the trees are bare. Straker believed the main pond was too small to power a furnace efficiently. There are some impressive rock formations here including the famous "Big Upon Little Rock" by the path up to the road. No parking.

Another, longer, footpath runs between here and West Hoathly, past Philpots in Chiddinglye Woods, leading to the charming fifteenth century Priest House, which has some local iron domestic items (see Museums below). The seventeenth century clockworks on view in St Margaret's church are said to have been donated by a local iron family. There are three grave slabs here for the Infield family, East Grinstead ironmasters who lived at local Gravetye Manor, two mounted on the south wall, and once standing in the chancel. Limited parking in West Hoathly by the church, or in the car park by the sports field 200 yards south.

Gravetye Furnace was established relatively late by William Clutton around 1760, and probably the last new furnace to be built in the Sussex Weald. It operated in conjunction with Warren Furnace but was demolished by 1787. Gravetye Furnace Pond (366342) was damaged after the ironworks closed and is now submerged under the modern Lower Lake by Gravetye Manor, now a hotel

Chithurst, near Trotton
SU 846236
Ex 133
PV

Peter Bettesworth managed Chithurst Forge, once also known as Iping Forge, circa 1632. A muddy bridleway leads north from a stile by the bridge in Hammer Lane to the pond, alongside the Hammer stream, leading further into Hammer Wood for about two miles north-east. The stream runs south from Chithurst Forge's associate **Milland Furnace Pond** (see below). Take care: the path by the pond was very slippery and unfenced at time of visit and the pond glimpsed only through trees and other undergrowth. One for robust enthusiasts only. The ruins of an Iron Age hill fort lie a short distance north of the pond. Hammer Lane is an easily missed track, leading east from Chithurst Lane, which turns north off the A272, just east of Trotton. Limited temporary parking opposite the stile.

Crabtree, Lower Beeding
TQ 228251
Ex 134
P
Station: Horsham

This pond lies within Leonardslee Woods, the lowest in a chain of ponds that served Gosden Furnace, operated by Roger Gratwick in 1580. The six pen ponds were later converted into ornamental lakes within Leonardslee Gardens, just north of the site. The furnace pond is near a footpath but currently fenced off on private land in woods, however the bay of its lowest pen pond, New Pond, can be reached via the same footpath north from the end of Mill Lane (no parking). This lane turns east off the A281, south of Lower Beeding near the Crabtree Inn; the footpath is slightly hilly and not easy walking.

Leonardslee Gardens in Lower Beeding were worth seeing, particularly when the famous rhododendrons were in bloom and reflected in the converted pen ponds. Unfortunately they were closed to the public in 2010, when the Loder family sold the property to a private company, and it is unknown whether they will reopen.

Old postcard of Gosden Furnace Pond, Crabtree.

Crawley Down

TQ 348393

Ex 135

PV

Station: Lingfield or East Grinstead

Originally known as Hedgecourt Furnace, this site was in 1574 leased by Edward Gage to John Thorpe, who managed it in conjunction with Gage's Woodcock Forge (see **Wire Mill**, and **Hedgecourt Lake** in Surrey, below), all of which belonged to the Gages' Manor of Hedgecourt. This ironworks, also known as Millwood but renamed Warren Furnace by 1758, supplied large and lucrative ordnance demands under Edward Raby's stewardship, but lay abandoned twenty years later. Warren Furnace Pond is now a private fishing lake, but a footpath passes along the bay in Furnace Wood, west of East Grinstead. There is an interesting stepped stone spillway (restored post-ironworks) on the path here. A field walker told me a group sensed the supernatural here one dusk, "as if the ghosts of old ironworkers were watching from behind trees". Mercifully, they left me alone when I visited.

The bay is about half a mile's walk along a footpath from the A264 near Snow Hill (no parking). It can also be approached from the opposite direction via the footpath north of Gibbshaven Bridge, on Furnace Farm Road west off the Felbridge Road (no parking). Part of this path runs along a private road with houses named Furnace, Forge and Hammer.

Ebernoe Furnace Pond, Kirdford

SU 974277

Ex 133

SSSI

ACC

Ebernoe Furnace Pond was established in 1594 by the Smythes of Wassell to make pig iron for Wassell Forge, at Kirdford. The waters are hidden in woodland on the large Ebernoe Common, an ancient woodland and nature reserve managed by the Sussex Wildlife Trust. A rugged wooded track between Ebernoe Church and the old schoolhouse leads downhill, past Furnace Meadow, to the pond.

Parking is available by the church, and on the common by the cricket pitch, a popular picnic site. More industrial relics from the eighteenth century can be found on the Common, including a limekiln at SU 972278, and brick moulding sheds at SU 979274. A 'Horn' Fair is held on the Common every July. Ebernoe lies on the minor road east of the A283 between Northchapel and Petworth: follow the signs to Ebernoe Church.

Fernhurst

SU 879283

Ex 133

ACC

The original furnace here was called North Park, operating by 1614 and leased by William Shotter. Pig iron made here supplied Pophole Forge in Surrey. Later, circa 1762, John Butler made cannon at this furnace, but it seems to have ceased work around

Fernhurst Furnace Pond from the northern sluice.

1777. The ore was dug from Minepit Copse and Furnace Wood, west and east of the pond respectively.

On the road leading west out of Fernhurst village, on the right (north) soon after Highbuilding one sees Greenhill House signed, a public footpath opposite (south) leads to the furnace pond through Furnace Wood. Alternatively, from the same road one could take the bridleway half a mile further west at Lower Lodge Farm.

Despite considerable water erosion this is probably the best-preserved ironworks site to view, in that some foundations of the furnace and tailrace remain and are clearly visible from the bay. These were extensively excavated and labelled by the current owners and the Fernhurst Society. Given recent flooding more conservation work is planned to rebuild and protect the bay and the bridleway atop it. An interesting book devoted to this furnace is available, compiled by John Magilton and others and published by Chichester District Council (see References and Further Reading below). It contains diagrams and artist's impressions of how furnace operations might have looked, as well as chapters on other local industrial history. The annual Fernhurst Furnace Open Day offers historical entertainments (including cannon firing) as well as detailed tours of this fascinating site. Parking is provided fairly close to the furnace bay at this time only. See www:fernhurstsociety.org.uk/furnace.html

Handcross
TQ 274294
Ex 134
NT
SSSI
ACC

Station: Balcombe

Blackfold Furnace Pond was established by Ninian Challoner in 1574. However the present bay at the grid reference above is a modern rebuild. The original furnace bay was yards downstream, and the working area below the eastern spillway. The furnace slagheap remains, now covered by grass.

Blackfold Furnace Pond, Handcross.

The pond now lies within Nymans Gardens, a National Trust property. Nymans has three woodland walk routes, including the Millennium Walk leading directly along the Furnace Pond bay. There are other lakes in the woods: Furnace Pond is the one with the old boathouse visible from the bay. Parking. Entrance fee. Walk maps are available from the Nymans Gardens shop. Tel: 01444 405250 for opening times, including wheelchair booking.

There is also a public footpath to the pond from Handcross village, through Cow Woods, which passes Nymans Gardens. Handcross lies off the B2110 south of Crawley.

Horsham
TQ 193292
Ex 134
PV
Station: Horsham

Birchenbridge Forge, originally owned by John Caryll in 1598, is not documented after 1627. The forge pond, later much enlarged, borders the busy A281 south of Horsham, and is now a private fishing lake. Roosthole Pond, upstream (204295), was probably a pen pond for the forge, fed by Sheepwash Ghyll in the ancient St Leonard's Forest. This is also a private fishing lake but there's a marvellous view from the footpath along Alders Copse. Join this path at Goldings Bridge at Goldings Lane, off Hammerpond Road. Roosthole can also be glimpsed from Hammerpond Road at 207297, where there is limited space for temporary parking. Nearby the Forestry Commission's Roosthole Car Park, slightly north in the Forest, has waymarked tracks and paths into the now mainly coniferous woods. This is near a site once known as 'roast hole' where the iron ore was roasted prior to charging the furnace. Roosthole could easily be combined with a trip on foot, or by car, to see the **St Leonard's Forest** ponds (below) further along the Hammerpond Road.

Old postcard of Birchenbridge Forge Pond, Horsham.

Horsted Keynes
TQ 379287
Ex 135
ACC
Station: Horsted Keynes (Bluebell Railway)

Beautiful Horsted Keynes Furnace Pond has an old corn mill with waterwheel nearby. During the mill's construction the original furnace site was flooded. William Barrantyne established the furnace circa 1544. The pond bay is on private land, but a footpath runs alongside the pond and past a modern spillway built over the original ironworks sluice.

The pond can be reached by either of two short parallel footpaths leading from the church of St Giles, down Church Lane. Combined, these form an attractive short circular walk, passing the mill and two smaller ponds. They also link with the Sussex Border Path north of the church, a trail that passes a chain of likely pen ponds although there is no firm evidence these served the furnace. A footpath also runs between the pond and the Bluebell Railway station about a mile away. Nearby Cinder Hill is named after a much earlier bloomery.

Ifield, near Crawley

TQ 245365

Ex 134

ACC

Station: Ifield

Ifield Forge Pond is set within an open public space. The footpath alongside extends to the (now dry) site of Bewbush Furnace Pond (TQ 239357), about a mile away. Sows from Bewbush were carried across to Ifield Forge by boat, or ox sled. Timber for charcoal was obtained from the surrounding Bewbush forest and deer park As the activities of the two sites were combined their history is confused: Thomas Fenner built Bewbush around 1569, but both Ifield and Bewbush were owned by Roger Gratwick in 1574. Ifield Forge was burned down by Cromwell's forces in 1643, together with other royalist ironworks nearby.

The railway bisects Ifield's huge pond, but this does not detract much from its beauty. The bay now supports a later corn mill, recently restored with a working water wheel. Ifield Mill has exhibitions on milling, iron working and other rural crafts and activities and is easily accessible at Hyde Drive, Ifield, just west of Crawley. Open on the last Sunday afternoon of the month from May to September, and on National Mills Day in May. Admission free. Souvenirs for sale. Donations welcome. Stair lift to first floor in mill. Small car park. Bay path partially wheelchair accessible – ring for details. Tel: Crawley Museum Society on 01293 539088.

Ifield – the modern mill on the bay.

Inholms Copse, near Milland

SU 850263

Ex 133

P

There is little documentary information about Inholms Copse Furnace but it is believed to be connected with Sir Peter Bettesworth's forge at **Chithurst**, circa 1632. The entire site including the working area suffered extensive damage during floods in 1968. Footpaths run nearby, from a minor road off Milland Lane to Titty Hill, but there is no public access to view the pond.

Milland, near Liphook

SU 832281

Ex 133

PV

Station: Liphook

Milland Furnace was established by Thomas Bettesworth around 1594 and supplied sows to his forge at Bramshott Hammer in Hampshire and possibly **Chithurst Forge** (see above). The pond can be glimpsed through trees from a footpath on a private track, east off Milland Lane just north of the village. This relatively small site is fed by numerous springs which must have provided a substantial power source, judging from the vigorously gushing spillway. A bridleway passes along the bay but beware the deep ford west across the track: the path is slippery and had a broken rail at time of visit. This stream runs down to **Chithurst Forge Pond**. Paths near Milland Furnace Pond eventually link up with the Sussex Border Path, slightly to the north. Milland Lane is an old Roman Road, just south of the B2070.

Burton Mill Pond, near Petworth
SU 979180
Ex 121
SSSI
ACC

Operated by William Goring in 1635, this was the most southerly of the West Sussex forges, supplied by several springs from the South Downs. This abundant water supply enabled the forge to thrive despite being relatively distant from furnaces. The bay of Burton Forge's spectacular hammer pond supports the Burton Park Road within a wooded nature reserve managed by the Sussex Wildlife Trust. The mill house later served a corn mill, and is now a restored private residence.

There is a small car park by the mill, and a footpath along the bay to a viewing platform. A trail to the west of the bay passes down the side of the pond, through Newpiece Wood. Burton Mill is occasionally open to the public on bank holidays: details from Sussex Mills Group (see Industrial History Societies below). Burton Park Road is signposted from the A285, about three miles south of Petworth.

Burton Forge Pond – the modern mill below the bay, on the old forge site.

Coombe Furnace Pond from the bay, Rake.

Rake
SU 815269
Ex 133
ACC
Station: Liss

Coombe Furnace, established circa 1589, was almost immediately leased to Henry Gleed and Michael Martin of Rogate. This great lake is visible from a sharp bend in Canhouse Lane where a short footpath leads to and around it. Do not confuse Coombe Pond with Cook's Pond further along the same road, which had nothing to do with the iron industry. Limited temporary parking by the footpath. Rake village is situated on the B2070.

Rowfant
TQ 316378
Ex 135
ACC
Station: Three Bridges

Robert Whitfield leased land and built a forge at Rowfant in 1556. This beautiful pond, now known as the Mill Pond, is accessible by footpath up to the bay along a private track east off Old Hollow road, which runs south off the A2220 below Copthorne. The original forge site is believed to be underneath 'Rowfant Studio'. No parking.

Rowfant Supra Forge Pond, operating around 1653, lies south east of the above in Horsepasture Wood (319372). This is currently back in water although marked as a dry antiquity on the OS map. No public access. There are two pen ponds for this forge upstream slightly further east in the grounds of nearby Elizabethan manor Rowfant House. Rowfant House is down Wallage Lane, which turns off the B2028. To combine a walk to all accessible ponds continue down the footpath from Rowfant Forge 'Mill' Pond, passing through Old Rowfant and down to Home Farm, where it joins the Sussex Border Path. This leads through woods to an imposing stone archway, part of Rowfant House.

Rudgwick
TQ 107333
Ex 134
PV

Dedisham Furnace was smelting by 1614 but there are no references to the ironworks after 1650. The pond has been restored and converted into private fishing lakes within a particularly peaceful setting. Furnace House, sited slightly east of the old pond bay, was the ironmaster's house, and later rebuilt with some of the furnace bricks.

The lakes are partially accessible either via a bridleway through the woods from Rowhook, or a footpath from Rudgwick: both link with a footpath alongside the top lake. Alternatively, a footpath north from the A281 west of Horsham leads up to the bay of the pond and over to Rudgwick, but this does not connect to the other paths around the lake above. Car park for anglers only.

St Leonard's Forest, near Mannings Heath
TQ 220290
Ex 134
SSSI
PV

Two extensive lakes shelter in parallel wooded valleys on Hammerpond Road, between Doomesday Green and Ashfold Crossway, divided by a small hill. Hammer Pond served St Leonard's Upper Forge; Hawkins Pond (216293) was a pen pond for the original Lower Forge and Furnace Pond, now dry. The forges are believed to have been constructed before 1561 and the furnace in 1584. These works were initially rented by the Gratwick family, then Edward Caryll in 1587, and the Caryll family gained ownership of the sites in 1601. Under Gratwick the furnace competed for ore with Gosden Furnace at **Crabtree** (above), leading to bad blood and legal and physical conflicts between the owners (Straker, 1931: 436–8). Both furnace and forges were ruined by 1664.

Hawkins Pond, St Leonard's Forest.

59

Each pond is about three-quarters of a mile in length but can only be viewed from the narrow, often busy country road. There is a small lay-by immediately beyond Hawkins Pond towards Doomsday Green, near a small orientation board which explains some of the iron industry's history. The Forestry Commission has a car park near Roosthole Pond (see **Horsham** above) – ideal if you wanted to combine a walk to all three ponds. Another option for a longer walk would be to park in Colgate village (231328) and walk about three miles south through the forest to Hammerpond Road: then turn left to the ponds.

The furnaces probably obtained ore from the northern area of the forest, towards Colgate, where there are mine pits. Local legend relates that St. Leonard slew a dragon that terrorised the forest; the famous lily of the valley beds (212308) mark the site. The beast managed to breed unfortunately, for a dragon was allegedly sighted there as late as 1614 (Bord & Bord, 1985: 67). A chapel dedicated to the saint once stood near Hawkins Pond. Carterslodge Pond, northeast at 243295 on Cartersledge Lane, was a pen pond for Hammer Pond.

Shillinglee, near Northchapel
SU 972308
Ex 133
SSSI
PV

This spectacular furnace pond was built by the lessee Thomas Smith in 1574, but closed by 1620. It later served a corn mill and the walled bay is now slightly higher than the original, while the furnace site is under Park Mill Farm. The pond can be reached by a footpath leading south from the Shillinglee Road east off the A283 above Northchapel. Shillinglee Lake is a few miles north of Ebernoe Furnace Pond (see above).

The Shillinglee Road also passes between two of the furnace's surviving pen ponds, Upper North and Lower North Ponds, at 963324 and 963321 by Shillinglee Park. These attractive lakes can easily be seen by the road, where there is limited parking in a lay-by.

Shillinglee Furnace Pond from the bay.

Shipley
TQ 157211
Ex 134
ACC

The Carylls, tenants of the Duke of Norfolk, operated Knepp Furnace circa 1568 to 1604. Now much larger than the original pond, the huge Knepp Mill Pond can be viewed from the foot-path running along a private track, Castle Lane, part of the Knepp Estate, which turns west off the busy A24. This track now forms a bay at the pond where the modern 'Y' shape of the lake becomes obvious. A sluice gate controls the spillway, which falls beneath the road to a stream back to the river Adur within a pic-turesque plain. The original furnace bay is thought to have been to the east by Floodgate Farm (163211).

Knepp Furnace Pond, Shipley.

No parking. Buses stop nearby on the busy A24. The ruins of the Norman Knepp Castle are just visible from the main road. For an alternative route to the furnace pond, join the footpath running roughly parallel to the Adur from Shipley village, half a mile away.

Half a mile south of Knepp, Shipley Forge Pond (149208) is recorded as dry, but now holds water although again a new bay confuses identification of the original working area. This is perhaps another 'reclaimed' pond. Little is known about Shipley Forge but it was functioning around 1615, probably worked in conjunction with Knepp Furnace above. The forge pond lies in the 'Hammer Pond' stream, which runs from Shipley to Hammer Farm, and can be reached from a footpath starting at the junction of Swallows Lane and Pound Lane. The bridge here crosses a stream with a large pool, but the pond is upstream of the pool and viewable only after a scramble up another, modern, bay.

Another local industrial history feature is Shipley windmill, a famous landmark and typical Sussex smock mill, once owned by the writer Hilaire Belloc. This has been restored and is open to the public occasionally on Sundays: details from Sussex Mills Group (see Industrial History Societies below). Shipley is on a minor road just south of the A272 below Horsham.

Slaugham
TQ 249282
Ex 134
SSSI
ACC
 on parking bay

Slaugham (pronounced Slaffam) Furnace was established by 1574 by Ninian Challoner and the local Covert family. This lovely pond is easily accessible on Slaugham Common, on Hampshire Hill Lane from Slaugham to Ashfold Crossways. The pond bay itself runs along this lane: turn right if coming from Slaugham to a small parking area on Coos Lane directly facing the water. There are paths from the parking spaces, some for

Slaugham Furnace Pond from the bay.

anglers only. Ashfold Lake, just north of here on private land (248286), may have been a pen pond. A dry ditch among hummocks in trees, on the west bay, the old working area, is thought to be the wheelpit – this is more or less visible depending on the season's overgrowth. Do not be misled by local references to an ornamental pond at nearby Slaugham Place, once home to the Coverts.

While you are here, you might want to scramble down to Our Ladies' Bowl. This chalybeate spring bubbles away down an unmarked track across the road from the east pond bay at roughly 247278. You may have to clear away leaves to see the bowl clearly, a sandstone basin installed over the spring in the seventeenth century by some Covert ladies to keep the water fresh. Its healing and restorative properties were still exercised in the early 1800s when it was collected for use as an eyewash, and has since been proven to possess similar elements to the Tunbridge Wells chalybeate spring (Ray, 1989: 11).

Warnham Mill Pond, near Horsham
TQ 170323
Ex 134
ACC Thurs to Sun, 10.00–1800/dusk

Station: Horsham

Warnham Furnace was constructed around 1609, and operated by John Caryll. An important cannon production site, annual draining and excavation for ironstone gradually enlarged the pond. However Parliamentarian forces destroyed the furnace during the Civil War. A few decades later the bay was converted to run a corn mill, which produced flour until the 1930s. The watermill building has recently been restored, and is private.

The pond has grown into a 17-acre lake within the 90-acre Warnham Nature Reserve, northwest of Horsham, on the B2237, just off the A24. Wildlife includes waterfowl, sedge, and willow warblers, and all species of woodpeckers, as well as dragonflies, damselflies, amphibians, reptiles and 200 species of wild plants. Parking. Visitor centre. Café. Guided walks. Some wheelchair access, including entry to bird hides. Small entry fee. Tel: 01403 256890 for details.

The poet Percy Bysshe Shelley was born at Field Place, near Warnham, and is said to have entertained his siblings with tales of a fabulous Great Tortoise in Warnham Mill Pond as well as the Dragon in St Leonard's Forest.

Warnham Furnace Pond.

East Sussex

Ashburnham, near Battle

TQ 685173

Ex 124

ACC/PV

This was an important Wealden ironwork complex of furnace, forges and boring mills, built by John Ashburnham around 1550, and the last Wealden furnace to close in 1813. The forge continued until the late 1820s. The sites worked together during the Civil War, and were the premier Wealden ordnance suppliers until about 1760, and later produced guns and shot for the Dutch Wars.

Ashburnham Upper Forge: wheelpit under house.

The main furnace pond is now dry, but a secluded pen pond survives on private land just north of the furnace site in Andersons Wood (685173). Several features remain here making a worthwhile and fascinating walk of about a mile altogether, starting from and returning to the hamlet of Ashburnham Forge.

An unmade road, heavily metalled with waste iron slag, runs about half a mile between the furnace's pen pond and the dry site of Ashburnham (Upper) Forge. Known as Sow Lane and originally as the 'sow track', this not only took sows and guns from the furnace down to the forge and boring mill but also extended up past Robertsbridge to Sedlescombe, where iron goods were shipped to London via the river Brede.

Rusty bears in the stream near Ashburnham Furnace.

The walk starts at a modern road over the bay of Ashburnham (Upper) Forge (687162) (limited parking). Part of the forge pond survives to the west by a road on private land at 684161, with a modern weir. However, from the bridge here, looking down eastwards, a rusty channel can clearly be seen far below, running under the conservatory of a house. This was the original tail-race and pit for the forge wheel.

Continue north by foot along the track (a bridleway) past wildflower meadows, glorious in summer, then take a detour at the path fork by following the bridleway to the right. Very shortly (685172) you will come to a footbridge over a ford with several large reddish 'bears' in the stream: waste slabs of imperfectly smelted ore and iron. Slightly further along, glancing left into the meadow you will see a high embankment, the old furnace bay. The furnace pond, now dry, lay beyond it. Depending on the time of year and vegetation, you should be able to see a brick section. This was the wheelpit area, now bricked up above the original arch which covers part of the narrow, dry pit remaining in the lower meadow. The old spill-way is a few yards along the bay and still serves a stream – again, depending on vegetation, the spillway may be seen as well as heard.

Retrace your steps back to the track fork and continue north to a terrace of old brick cottages adjacent to the furnace bay. The first, Furnace Cottage, locally known as Pay Cottage, has a small square window nearest the gate said to be where the ironworkers collected their wages. Past these cottages, slightly further up the track the other end of the pond bay is just visible (no public access). Continuing north you soon reach the furnace's pen pond on the left in Andersons Wood. These waters are on private land, but the red stream bottom is clearly visible from the bridge here, where a small spillway lets the stream run into the wood on the other side that was once part of the main furnace pond.

It is a short walk from here to the end of a minor road, Lakehouse Lane, at the end of the footpath, and you might spot another bear set into the ground to the right of Trinity Cottage gate. However, I recommend you walk back down to the Forge, unless you are including these sites within a much longer walk in the area: there are no villages nearby.

Ashburnham Forge is on a minor road off Penhurst Lane, from the A271 west of Battle. The long distance 1066 Country Walk passes through the hamlet. There is limited parking at Penhurst Church, next to the landmark manor house, marked as an antiquity on the OS map. Ashburnham parish church contains an iron screen made at the forge: there is a right of way to the church down the drive belonging to the private Ashburnham prayer centre. Car park opposite the church.

Young ironworker William Hobday often spoke of the end of the furnace's last campaign, as reported in his obituary much later in the *Sussex Express* in 1883. Sadly, he revealed that a six-year-old boy also present drank a whole bottle of gin, and was dead before the doctor came

'Pay' Cottage, Ashburnham.

(SIAS, 1983: 3). Rumour holds that the fire was extinguished prematurely, after neglect due to inebriation. One of the last products was a fireback for the Ashburnham family.

Buxted
TQ 477272
Ex 135
P

Oldlands Furnace Pond still holds water on private land north of Furnace Woods in the hamlet of Heron's Ghyll, northwest of Buxted. No public access. William Basset operated the furnace in 1593, possibly in conjunction with Crowborough Forge. It was leased out at least until 1617.

It's often claimed that Ralph Hogge worked this site, but there is no evidence of this. Hogge was the colleague and successor of Peter Baude, who cast the first one-piece cast-iron cannon, at Queenstock furnace near Iron Plat. Hogge's iron rebus, or personal stamp, is above the door at the entrance to Buxted Park, a few miles south of here.

Eridge
TQ 568344
Ex 135
P
Station: Eridge

John Waller owned Hamsell Furnace until his death in 1567, when it was occupied and operated by John Baker. By 1692 it was producing shells, ceasing around 1750. The furnace was demolished by 1787. The bay area has since been landscaped and the much-altered lake is on private land, but you can just glimpse the waters through trees by a gate on a footpath. This path runs south from Forge Road, a minor road near Eridge railway station west off the A26, between Eridge Green and Boarshead. The site is not far from a spring fed cattle trough which cascades into the road; another pond on the north side is unrelated to the iron industry.

Eridge Green, near Frant
TQ 564350
Ex 135
SSSI
ACC/PV
Station: Eridge

There are records of French workers, presumably skilled blast furnace operators, at Eridge Furnace since 1538. Lord Abergavenny owned it in 1574, together with a forge nearby. This is one of the bigger ponds, set in woodlands, with pen ponds upstream. The High Weald Landscape Trail runs along the former bay between this huge lake and a pen pond, near a sluice. You can join the trail at a public footpath west off the A267 just below Frant village. Some street parking is available in Frant. The church here has seventeenth century iron memorial slabs for the Fowles, a local iron family, in the aisle, but these are now covered by carpet.

Framfield (east)/Blackboys
TQ 515211
Ex: 123
ACC

Tickerage Forge and Furnace Pond are believed to have existed at separate times due to the restricted space. Records suggest the forge functioned from around 1617 to 1664 in what is now the mill house garden. This is one of the smaller ponds within a peaceful scenic setting with several interesting features. The original spillway and millrace remain on the bay, with a ferruginous stream running through the leat of the later corn mill building opposite the pond. An iron mould for making cannon balls was found here. Tickerage Mill belongs to the nearby house, one of the last homes of actor Vivien Leigh, whose ashes were scattered on this estate.

The bay lies east along the Wealdway long distance path as it crosses off Pound Lane, north of the B2102 between Framfield and Blackboys. The path is shared at this point with the Vanguard Way route from Poundgate to Blackboys. Pounsley Furnace, eastwards along Tickerage Stream, was also a major cannon producer. The old gun banks for test firing new cannon survive at Pounsley Mill Farm, but the pond is now dry.

Framfield (south)

TQ 509195

Ex 123

PV

Station: Uckfield

This is believed to be the site of New Place Furnace, circa 1560, but it has been extensively altered and landscaped. There is an interesting chain of ponds and spillways along the stream on private land but viewable from the Wealdway long distance path leading east off Pump Lane, which runs south of the B2102 between Framfield and Blackboys. Blackboys got its name from the local charcoal burners, then known as 'wood colliers'.

The Framfield sites are close enough to easily combine a visit by road and/or the Wealdway path.

New Place Furnace Pond, Framfield.

Furners Green
TQ 416257
Ex 135
ACC
Station: Sheffield Park (Bluebell Railway)

Sheffield Furnace was established by 1546 but converted to a corn mill by 1597. An impressive spillway in the middle of the pond bay is probably original. The bay sits on a footpath along a private track running east from the bottom of Tanyard Lane in the hamlet of Furners Green just east of the A275 between Danehill and North Chailey. Limited temporary parking opposite the track entrance. Paths lead from the bay to Sheffield Forest, or

Sheffield Furnace Pond from the bay.

75

alternatively to Ketches Lane near Fletching. Sheffield Corn Mill was later built over the furnace area and is sometimes open to the public on National Mills Weekend, usually held in May: contact SIAS for details.

Sheffield Park Gardens' ornamental lakes, to the south, have no connection with the furnace or forge.

Heathfield
TQ 594196
Ex 123
P

John Fuller of Brightling built Heathfield Furnace in 1693. He was a primary ordnance supplier to Ireland, Sardinia and Naples as well as the British government: two of his guns stand by the Tower of London. The ironworks ceased production in 1793. The furnace pond was near the hamlet of Old Heathfield, but has since been drained and the bay damaged. A chain of four pen ponds survives upstream within the private Heathfield Park. Originally there were twelve according to a 1795 estate map (C&C, 1995: 335), presumably necessary due to local watershed difficulties.

Another small pen pond survives together with part of the old brick spillway at TQ 594196, down a muddy public footpath. Nearby All Saints Church contains two plain iron grave slabs. Old Heathfield can be reached by travelling west along the B2096 road, turning right down School Hill just before Cade Street. John Fuller's great-grandson was the infamous 'Mad Jack' Fuller, who built several follies around the Brightling area.

Herstmonceux

TQ 632153

Ex 124

P

Lessees Thomas Glydd and Simon Colman built Batsford Furnace on what was then the Batsford Brook here in 1571, north of Herstmonceux. This is one of the 'reclaimed' ponds, dry for many years since the stream breached the original bay. A new bay was constructed close to the old site during landscaping in the late 1970s, and the pond excavated and refilled for a new fish farm. It is now a private fishing lake, Furnace Brook Fishery, on New Road northeast from Cowbeech.

Maresfield

TQ460228

Ex 135

ACC

Station: Uckfield

Maresfield Forge was established by John Gage and worked from before 1574 until about 1787. For some time the forge supplied a shop in Lewes High Street with bar iron and tools. This much-altered lake, at the end of a chain of smaller ponds, was used by a powder mill in the nineteenth century. It is on private land, but a footpath runs alongside from the churchyard in Maresfield village, about a mile north (where there is a car park at the sports ground). An iron grave slab for Robert Brooks is stored in the tower of St Bartholomew's Church. Budletts Common nearby is almost certainly associated with the local iron industry: 'budlett' was a place-name for a site where iron ore was washed (Straker, 1931: xii).

Riverhall, near Wadhurst/Frant

TQ 605333

Ex 136

PV

Station: Wadhurst

Riverhall Furnace was operated by Nicholas Fowle in 1562, and last worked in 1653. The furnace was within the grounds of Riverhall Mansion, constructed by the prosperous Fowle in 1591. Two pen ponds survive by Partridges Lane, which runs south off the B2099, about a mile northwest of Wadhurst railway station. Only one, at the GR above, is clearly visible from the road, which crosses a small ferruginous stream just before the pond. No parking.

Riverhall pond is probably not worth visiting unless you are already in the area. A footpath from here passes an old bay at 602336 within Furnace Woods, judged to be the site of Henly Lower Furnace, before joining the Sussex Border Path at Lightlands. The small pond to the east is thought to be a mine-pit.

Scarlets Lake, near Cowden
TQ 443401
Ex 147
ACC
Station: Cowden (approx 2 miles)

This pond, once dry but restored in 1977, powered Scarlets Furnace for Francis Knight in 1590. A gun-casting pit was uncovered here at the site of the old furnace at the north end of the bay. The site was still in service in the 1690s making ordnance, and suffered a broken bay in the great storm of 1703. This was rebuilt but a decade or two later the site was converted into a corn mill.

The bay of Scarlets Furnace Pond, near Cowden.

Scarlets Furnace Pond lies on a bridleway south from Smithers Lane by the border between East Sussex and Kent, near Hammerwood, just west of **Cowden Furnace Pond** (see Kent below). The bridleway passes over the bay of the pond, and an old ruined sluice lies on the south of the bay. A few products from both of these furnaces are on display at the Eden Valley Museum (see Museums below).

Smithers Lane turns east off Shepherds Grove Lane, which runs north from the A264 west of Holtye. Only temporary parking by this pond, on a narrow road. Limited parking is available in a lay-by just east of the White Horse inn at Holtye (459393) from which you could make a circular trip to take in two ponds. Walk a mile north along the footpath from there up past Holtye Common to the Cowden pond, and then on west along Furnace Lane (which becomes Smithers Lane) to Scarlets. The bridleway here will take you south through Mill Wood back to the A264, about a mile west of the pub.

Bower Forge was in the grounds of what is now the Hammerwood Park Estate (441384) but the pond is long gone since landscaping transformed the area. The ponds downstream from the forge site are ornamental and unconnected with the forge. There's an iron memorial for ironmaster 'John Bottinge of the Bower' (Forge, near East Grinstead), dated 1622, inside the church at Cowden.

Kent

Fewer ironworks ponds survive in Kent, but the High Weald villages of Biddenden, Cranbrook, Goudhurst, Hawkhurst, Lamberhurst, as well as those below, were all involved in the industry.

Bayham, near Lamberhurst
TQ 642366
Ex 136
P

William Wybarne leased the Abbey Forge circa 1520, and it was still operating in 1667. The pond, heavily silted up, still holds water by the river Teise south of Forge Wood, within the private Bayham Estate, on the Kent and Sussex border east of Bayham Abbey. Rudyard Kipling mentions the forge in Puck's Song from his Puck of Pook's Hill:

> *And mark you where the ivy clings*
> *To Bayham's mouldering walls?*
> *O there we cast the stout railings*
> *That stand around St Paul's.*

Yet, as stated above, these were made just downstream at Gloucester Furnace in Lamberhurst, Kent (TQ 662360).

Cowden

TQ 454400

Ex 147

ACC

Station: Cowden

The bay of the extensive Cowden Furnace Pond lies on Furnace Lane, below Cowden village, bisected by the county boundaries of Kent and Sussex. The furnace was in Kent, but the waterwheel in Sussex. It was established in the late sixteenth century, and William Bowen was the last known owner of the site, until 1771.

Furnace Lane lies west off Holtye Hill, which runs north from the A264 at Holtye. There is a small space for temporary parking on an unmarked path adjacent to the south end of the bay, by the road. Limited parking is also available in a lay-by east of the

Cowden Furnace Pond from the bay.

82

White Horse inn south at Holtye (459393) where footpaths will take you about half a mile up past Holtye Common to the pond.

There's an iron memorial to John Bottinge, dated 1622, within Mary Magdalene Church in Cowden village, in the floor before the pulpit, part covered by a pew. Two rusty iron grave slabs for Richard and Mary Still, who died in 1726 and 1730 respectively, lie outside in the churchyard near the vestry door.

Scarlets Furnace Pond (see East Sussex, above) lies about a mile west along the same lane. A few relics from both of these furnaces are on display at the Eden Valley Museum (see Museums below). You could make a circular trip on foot to take in two ponds by walking from the White Horse north to Cowden pond, and then west along Furnace Lane to **Scarlets**. The bridleway here will take you south through Mill Wood back to the A264, about a mile west of the pub.

Horsmonden
TQ 695412
Ex 136
ACC
Station: Paddock Wood

Horsmonden Furnace, also known as Brenchley, was established before 1574. It was mainly used for gun casting and was still operating circa 1667. Local gun founder John Browne was Crown ordnance supplier. He made guns for Charles I, and later for Cromwell's Commonwealth. Horsmonden's ordnance products were despatched to the River Medway and then shipped on to London. The present Horsmonden village grew up around the furnace and foundry sites, most of which lie within the parish of Brenchley.

This spectacular pond, rightly called a 'fine sheet of water' by Straker, is about a quarter of a mile in length. A footpath from Furnace Lane leads to the bay, part of the High Weald Landscape Trail. The footbridge here passes over a spillway whose waters gush down stone tiers to what was formerly the furnace site beneath the bay, now the famous 'Horsmonden Waterfall'. Depending on the water level and overgrowth a large bear can be seen isolated in a midstream pool here; however the path down to view this feature is hazardous, one for the robust, accompanied, seeker only.

Horsmonden lies on the B2162: Furnace Lane turns north off the Brenchley Road near the post office: after about 500 yards there is a small lay-by providing limited temporary parking by

Horsmonden Furnace Pond, from the bay.

View down the spillway at the bridge, Horsmonden Furnace Pond bay.

the footpath to the pond. Alternatively one could join the above trail by the pond by walking approx 1½ miles from Brenchley village, where there is public parking; the path turns off the road just south of the Halfway House pub.

A plain iron slab with brass memorial plate commemorates John Browne's wife Martha under the chancel arch at St Margaret's Church, about a mile south in the original Horsmonden village at TQ 704383.

Wealden cannon outside the Sergeant's House and Gaol, High Street, New Romney.

Surrey

Abinger Hammer

TQ 097474

Ex 145

Conservation Area

PV

 by shop car park

Station: Gomshall

There are few visible remains now of the forge pond on Tilling-bourne stream that powered Abinger Hammer (formerly known as Shere) Forge, long converted into watercress beds and so considerably lower than the original bay and water level.

The watercress ponds at Abinger Hammer after harvest.

I include this site because Abinger Forge was the most northerly site of the Wealden iron industry, built before 1557 by Owen Bray. There were no furnaces nearby due to lack of suitable local ore, so this forge converted iron sows from Sussex into wrought-iron. It was still operating circa 1751 when John Goodyer occupied the works and supplied his family's ironmonger business in Guildford. Alexander Raby, who had also established iron mills on Surrey's Wey and Mole rivers, was the last known owner of Abinger Hammer in 1787.

What's left of the former chain of forge ponds are best viewed from the farm shop on the original bay site, just off the main road, perhaps worth visiting if you are in the area. The 'old forge hole', assumed to be remains of the wheelpit, can be seen by the entrance to the car park here. The village is midway between Guildford and Dorking off the A25, near Gomshall railway station. Shere Museum nearby has a small mechanical model of the forge hammer.

Hedgecourt Lake, Felbridge

TQ 360404

Ex 146

SSSI

ACC

♿ on parking bay

Station: Lingfield or East Grinstead

This huge sheet of water, 42 acres, was used as a pen pond for Woodcock Hammer Forge (approx 1574 onwards) at **Wire Mill Lake** below. It continued in use as a reservoir to provide back-up power for subsequent mills there. This is not the site of Hedge-court Furnace, the original name of Warren Furnace, at **Crawley Down**, above: both sites belonged to the Manor of Hedgecourt. The lake lies within a Surrey Wildlife Trust nature reserve near Felbridge. This lake can be hard for drivers to find, lying down Mill Lane, a minor road north off the A264 between Felbridge and Copthorne. There is designated parking on the bay facing the pond, making some wheelchair access possible. The footpath from here to **Wire Mill Lake** (see below) crosses the A22.

Thursley Common, near Hindhead
SU 915402
Ex 145
NT
SSSI
ACC
Station: Witley

There are three forge ponds in the Thursley Common nature reserve area, connected with Thursley and Witley Forges, first mentioned in 1608. The Upper Hammer pond at the GR above is near the A3 southwest of Milford. A bridleway from a small lay-by on this road leads to the pond. A guide map here details various trails and the site of the hammer pond, which has a bridge and a small spillway. The original bay, at 916403, is not easily accessible through the trees and undergrowth. The pond is fed by a stream running (north) through a chain of ponds from Hindhead Common, and in turn feeds the (restored) Lower Hammer Pond at 916408. This mill was later reused for silk.

Just north of here Coldharbour Hammer Pond (920406) runs on a different stream east of the other hammer ponds, and lies partly in Thursley and partly in Witley. Footpaths run alongside all these ponds. Parking and Visitor Centre on Witley Common. Tel: 01428 681050.

Nearby Warren Mere lake was not connected to the ironworks: the channel running between the Mere and the hammer ponds was constructed in the nineteenth century (C&C, 1995: 260). There was a Witley Park Furnace further south at 927374 circa 1673, but the pond is long gone.

Wire Mill Lake, Newchapel
TQ 367418
Ex 146
ACC
Station: Lingfield or East Grinstead

Wire Mill Lake, towards the bay.

This impressive lake was formerly the pond for Woodcock Hammer Forge, and straddles the Eden Brook. John Thorpe worked this forge by 1574, in conjunction with Hedgecourt, later Warren, Furnace in Cuttinglye Wood, Crawley Down nearby in Sussex (see above). It reputedly made the nails for St Paul's Cathedral and by the late eighteenth century operated as a wire mill.

The building has been restored as an inn and restaurant on the pond bay, with a waterwheel preserved on the side of the mill. The inn is said to be haunted by a former mill worker who fell into the machinery, whose body was not recovered until many years later. This pond lies at the end of Wire Mill Lane, east off the A22 in Newchapel. Parking by the public footpath alongside the lake. This path makes a pleasant walk along to this site's former pen pond **Hedgecourt Lake** (see above) about a mile away.

Iron mortar bowl cast at Brede (by kind permission of Hastings Museum and Art Gallery. Now in storage).

Museums

Anne of Cleves House Museum

52 Southover Street, Lewes, East Sussex BN7 1JA

Tel: 01273 474610

A must. This museum, owned by the Sussex Archaeological Society, houses the best and most informative exhibition of Wealden iron. It includes a number of iron firebacks, wooden stamps, cannon and smaller items such as fire-dogs, and large pieces of surviving machinery including part of Chingley Forge waterwheel, a hammer from Etchingham Forge, and a boring bar. Open Mon–Sat, April–October. Ring for times during other months.

http://www.sussexpast.co.uk/

Boring apparatus, Anne of Cleves House Museum (by kind permission of the Sussex Archaeological Society).

Ashdown Forest Centre

Ridge Road, Wych Cross, Forest Row, East Sussex RH18 5JP
Tel: 01342 823583
This visitor centre includes a small display about the local iron industry, including information about the first documented blast furnaces in Britain. Open every afternoon April until October, weekends and bank holidays only during winter.
http://www.ashdownforest.org/about/forest_centre.php

Battle Museum of Local History

The Almonry, High Street, Battle, East Sussex TN33 OEA
01424 775955
Exhibitions are varied here but there are always a few items from the blast furnace period including cannon balls from Brede and Robertsbridge Furnaces, part of a shattered Brede cannon, and some early bloomery items. Some larger items such as a vat and mortar, also cast at Brede, are due to be put on display in due course. Open Mon–Sat, Sunday afternoons, April to end October.
http://www.battlemuseum.org.uk

Eden Valley Museum

Church House, High Street, Edenbridge, Kent TN8 5AR
01732 868102
There is a Wealden iron display and some artefacts here, including cannonballs from Cowden and Scarlets Furnaces and sections of the railings from St Paul's Cathedral, cast at Kent's Gloucester Furnace, Lamberhurst. However, displays can vary so ring for details.
Open: Tues–Sat, Sundays in winter.

Guildford Museum
Castle Arch, Guildford, Surrey GU1 3SX
Tel: 01483 444751
This museum possesses several firebacks, plus a changing selection of items relating to the industry.
http://www.guildford.gov.uk/museum

Haslemere Educational Museum
78 High Street, Haslemere, Surrey GU27 2LA
Tel: 01428 642112
The history gallery has a small display relating to Wealden industries, including samples of slag and pig iron, and a few iron artefacts include a 'date plate' of 1564 featuring Elizabeth I, and an iron statuette of a priest discovered at Passfield Mill – a relic of Bramshott Hammer. Most displays are accessible by wheelchair; however phone first for parking/access assistance. Open Tues–Sat.
http://www.haslemeremuseum.co.uk/

Horsham Museum
9 The Causeway, Horsham, West Sussex RH12 1HE
Tel: 01403 254959
There is a small display of iron artefacts here, including firebacks, cannon balls and domestic utensils, in a case on the ground floor. A couple of 18th century cannon, cast at Brede Furnace, are outside in the courtyard. Open Mon–Sat.
http://www.horshammuseum.org/

Priest House
North Lane, West Hoathly, West Sussex RH19 4PP
Tel: 01342 810479
Now owned by the Sussex Archaeological Society, this beautiful fifteenth century timber-framed farmhouse has a small exhibition on Wealden iron, locally produced cannon balls, a few firebacks, two of which may be Dutch, and innumerable domestic items including a salamander and firedogs. An iron slab, possibly a bear from a local furnace, is inlaid at the doorstep for good luck: folklore maintained these could repel witches. Open March to end October. Limited wheelchair access.
http://www.sussexpast.co.uk/

Ripley Museum of Rural Life
Mark Ripley Antiques and Forge,
Northbridge Street, Robertsbridge, East Sussex
Tel: 01580 880324
This forge and fireplace manufacturer reproduces period firebacks, andirons etc and has a vast collection of mostly original seventeenth and eighteenth century firebacks, providing some idea of the variety of designs used. Museum of rural industry attached. Phone for opening times.

Royal Armouries Artillery Museum
Portsdown Hill Road, Fort Nelson, Fareham,
Hampshire PO17 6AN
Tel: 01329 233734
This museum has several examples of Wealden ordnance. Open daily April–October, Thurs–Sun 10.30–4.00 during winter months.
http://www.royalarmouries.org/

Royal Armouries Museum
Armouries Drive, Leeds LS10 1LT
Tel: 0113 220 1999
Some Wealden cannon are displayed in the Hall of Steel staircase here. Open daily.
http://www.royalarmouries.org/

Rural Life Centre
Reeds Road, Tilford, Farnham, Surrey
Tel: 01252 795571
This centre has built a half-scale replica blast furnace, with bellows and waterwheel. For demonstration purposes a half-scale helve hammer has also been attached to the wheel. An experimental smelt a few years ago succeeded in producing a small quantity of pig iron. More smelts are planned for the future once adequate supplies of charcoal and storage are available. Volunteers are needed and are welcome to join this fascinating project, including the preparation of charcoal and roasting of ore, before smelting is attempted. Contact Gerald Baker at the above phone number for details. The museum is open March to the end of October, ring for winter opening times.
http://www.rural-life.org.uk

Model of blast furnace bellows and waterwheel (by kind permission of the Rural Life Centre, Tilford).

The loading platform on the roof of the replica furnace (by kind permission of the Rural Life Centre, Tilford).

Tunbridge Wells Museum
Civic Centre, Mount Pleasant, Tunbridge Wells, Kent TN1 1JN
Tel: 01892 554171
This small exhibition includes a model of a water-driven hammer forge and the usual iron artefacts. There is also a small cannon, or falconet, cast by John Fuller at Heathfield, some shot dug up at Yalding, and a couple of railings from St Paul's Cathedral. Open Mon–Sat, except bank holidays.
http://www.tunbridgewellsmuseum.org/http://www.haslemeremuseum.co.uk/

'Scissors and Knives' 16th century fireback, Anne of Cleves House Museum (by kind permission of the Sussex Archaeological Society).

Industrial History Societies

Wealden Iron Research Group
WIRG, established in 1968, is the leading organisation undertaking and publishing research into historical iron production in the High Weald. Activities include archaeological forays, excavations, bloomery experiments and biennial general meetings. More information including an extensive online iron site database, publications and membership forms is available from: www.wealdeniron.org.uk/

The following relevant groups produce regular bulletins and journals; given periodic changes in contact details only web addresses are included here.

Historical Metallurgy Society
http://www.hist-met.org/

Kent Archaeological Society
http://www.kentarchaeology.org.uk/

Surrey Industrial History Group
http://www.sihg.org.uk/

Sussex Archaeological Society / Sussex Past
http://www.sussexpast.co.uk/

Sussex Industrial Archaeology Society
http://www.sussexias.co.uk/

Sussex Mills Group
http://www.sussexmillsgroup.org.uk/

References and Further Reading

Bacher, P. M. *Ifield Water Mill: Its Owners and Occupiers*, Crawley Museum Society Publication No 3, 1994

Barter Bailey, S. *Prince Rupert's Patent Guns*, Leeds, Royal Armouries, 2000

Beswick, M. *Ironworking in Warbleton*, Warbleton & District History Group No 15, 2003

Binnie, G. M. *Early dam builders in Britain*, London, Thomas Telford, 1987

Bord, J. & Bord, C. *The Secret Country*, London, Paladin, 1985

Brandon, P. & Short, B. *The Southeast From AD 1000*, London, Longman, 1990

Brown, R. R. "Identifying 18th-century trunnion marks on British iron guns: a discussion", *International Journal of Nautical Archaeology and Underwater Exploration*, Volume 18.4: 321–329, 1989

Cleere, H. & Crossley, D. *The Iron Industry of the Weald*, Cardiff, Merton Priory Press, 1995

Crocker, G. *A Guide to the Industrial Archaeology of Surrey*, Association for Industrial Archaeology, 1990

Crocker, G., Ed. *Alexander Raby, Ironmaster,* Guildford, Surrey Industrial History Group, 2000

Defoe, D. *A Tour Through the Whole Island of Great Britain,* Harmondsworth, Penguin, 1986

Edwards, S. *Children of the Weald,* Edwards, 1996

Haslefoot, A. J. *The Batsford Guide to the Industrial History of South-East England,* London, Batsford, 1978

Henbery, E. W. *Ifield Watermill Restoration,* Crawley Museum Society, 1996

Herbert, B. K. *The Field Walker's Guide & Introduction to the Iron Industries of the Weald,* WIRG, 1985

Herbert, B. K. & Cornish, T. "The Location of Etchingham Forge", *Wealden Iron,* 2nd Series No 32: 28-35, WIRG, 2012

Hodgkinson, J. & Houghton, R. "Iridge Furnace, Hurst Green", *Wealden Iron,* 2nd Series No 20: 32-39, WIRG, 2000

Hodgkinson, J. *The Wealden Iron Industry,* The History Press, 2008

Hodgkinson, J. *British Cast-Iron Firebacks,* hodgersbooks, 2010

Hunnisett, R. *Sussex Coroners' Inquests, 1603–88,* Public Record Office, Kew, 1998

Magilton, John et al. *Fernhurst Furnace,* Chichester District Council, 2003

Manwaring Baines, J. *Wealden Firebacks,* Hastings Museum, 1958

Ray, R. *Around Old Slaugham,* 1989

Riden, P. *A Gazetteer of Charcoal fired Blast Furnaces in Great Britain in use since 1660,* Cardiff, Merton Priory Press, 1993

Sargent, George E. *Hurlock Chase; or, Among the Sussex Ironworks,* 1876, Religious Tract Society

Straker, E. *Wealden Iron,* London, Bell and Sons Ltd, 1931, reprinted Bath, Cedric Chivers Ltd, 1967

SIAS *Sussex Industrial Archaeology Society Newsletter No 39,* July 1983

Tadd, M. *A Guide to the Industrial History of Tandridge,* Surrey Industrial History Group, 1994

Teesdale, E.B. *Gunfounding in the Weald in the Sixteenth Century,* London, HM Tower of ondon Royal Armouries Monograph 2, 1991

Wright, P. *Frant, the Story of a Wealden Parish,* Committee of Frant Publications Project, 1982

Zell, M. *Industry in the Countryside: Wealden Society in the Sixteenth Century,* (Cambridge Studies in Population, Economy and Society in Past Time), Cambridge University Press, 1994

Glossary

Ancony   A short thick iron bar from a finery or chafery, with unwrought ends.

Bay   A raised clay dam or embankment built across a stream to create an artificial pond.

Bear   A large lump of imperfectly smelted ore and cast-iron, left when a furnace is blown out, or extinguished.

Bloom   A bar of crude wrought-iron produced in a bloomery or finery forge (from the Old English *bloma*, or lump).

Bloomery   Earliest type of furnace, also known as the 'direct' process.

Boring   Smoothing the bore of cannon with a boring bar, also known as reaming.

Cascabel   The rounded projection behind the breech of a cannon.

Chafery   A forge which converts wrought-iron blooms into iron bars.

Chalybeate   Highly ferruginous spring waters, once believed to be medicinal.

Cinder   Solid waste residue produced during smelting.

Coppicing   Periodical cutting of saplings from the same rootstock to conserve wood supplies.

Ferruginous   Containing iron (eg streams) or rust-coloured.

Finery   A forge which converts bar iron into crude wrought iron.

Furnace   Nowadays used to refer to a powered 'blast' furnace.

Ghyll	A steep narrow valley with a rapid stream.
Iron ore	Rock containing iron.
Leat	A channel taking water to the mill wheel.
Marl	Alkaline clay once excavated for use as a soil improver.
Mine	Archaic term for iron ore. It does not refer to mine-pit craters.
Pen Pond	A supplementary 'feeder' reservoir, upstream of the main pond.
Pig	Lump or length of cast-iron.
Reaming	See Boring, above.
Rebus	Personal or trade stamp/mark.
Slag	Solid furnace waste residue.
Sluice	Gate or hatch to regulate water flow.
Smelting	The extraction of iron from iron ore via intense heat.
Sow	Length of cast-iron, larger than a pig, up to half a ton.
Stamp	Carved wooden design pressed into sand to make a mould for cast-iron.
Spillway	A channel to relieve overflow from the pond, usually with stepped masonry to dissipate the force of this water.
Trunnion	A pivot that projects from each side of a cannon to enable it to turn.
Tuyere	Clay nozzles at the base of a furnace for the insertion and protection of wooden air pipes to the leather bellows.

Index